Our Beautiful Garden

Saving Our Planet

This is our garden.

3

We have trees in our garden.

We have birds in our garden.

We have flowers in our garden.

9

We have **bees**
in our garden.

We have **water** in our garden.

We have **frogs** in our garden.

15

bees

frogs

water